INVENTIONS AND DISCOVERY

Henry Ford and the MODEL T

by Michael O'Hearn

illustrated by Phil Miller,
Keith Wilson, and Charles Barnett III

Consultant:
Frank Gasiorek, PhD
Henry Ford Estate–Fair Lane
University of Michigan
Dearborn, Michigan

Capstone
press
Mankato, Minnesota

Graphic Library is published by Capstone Press,
151 Good Counsel Drive, P.O. Box 669, Mankato, Minnesota 56002.
www.capstonepress.com

Printed in the United States of America

1 2 3 4 5 6 11 10 09 08 07 06

Library of Congress Cataloging-in-Publication Data
O'Hearn, Michael, 1972–
Henry Ford and the Model T / by Michael O'Hearn; illustrated by Phil Miller, Keith Wilson, and Charles Barnett III.
p. cm.—(Graphic library. Inventions and discovery)
Summary: "In graphic novel format, tells the story of Henry Ford and his popular Model T automobile"—Provided by publisher.
Includes bibliographical references and index.
ISBN-13: 978-0-7368-6480-0 (hardcover)
ISBN-10: 0-7368-6480-6 (hardcover)
ISBN-13: 978-0-7368-9642-9 (softcover pbk.)
ISBN-10: 0-7368-9642-2 (softcover pbk.)
1. Ford, Henry, 1863–1947—Juvenile literature. 2. Automobile engineers—United States—Biography—Juvenile literature. 3. Businessmen—United States—Biography—Juvenile literature. 4. Ford Model T automobile—Juvenile literature. 5. Ford Motor Company—Juvenile literature. I. Title. II. Series.
TL140.F6O38 2007
338.7'629222092—dc22 2006008187

Designer
Bob Lentz

Colorist
Melissa Kaercher

Editor
Christopher Harbo

TABLE OF CONTENTS

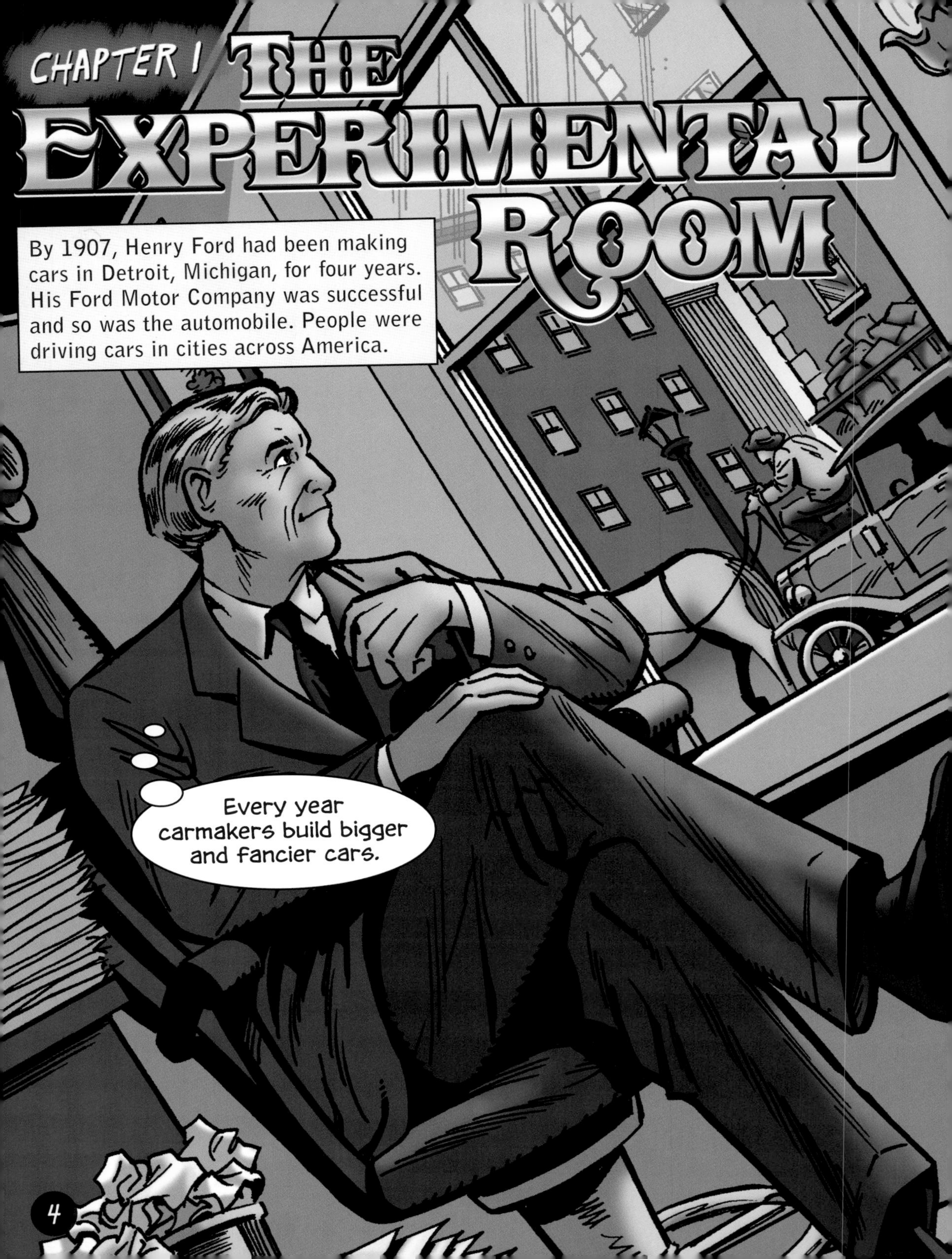
CHAPTER 1 THE EXPERIMENTAL ROOM
By 1907, Henry Ford had been making cars in Detroit, Michigan, for four years. His Ford Motor Company was successful and so was the automobile. People were driving cars in cities across America.
Every year carmakers build bigger and fancier cars.

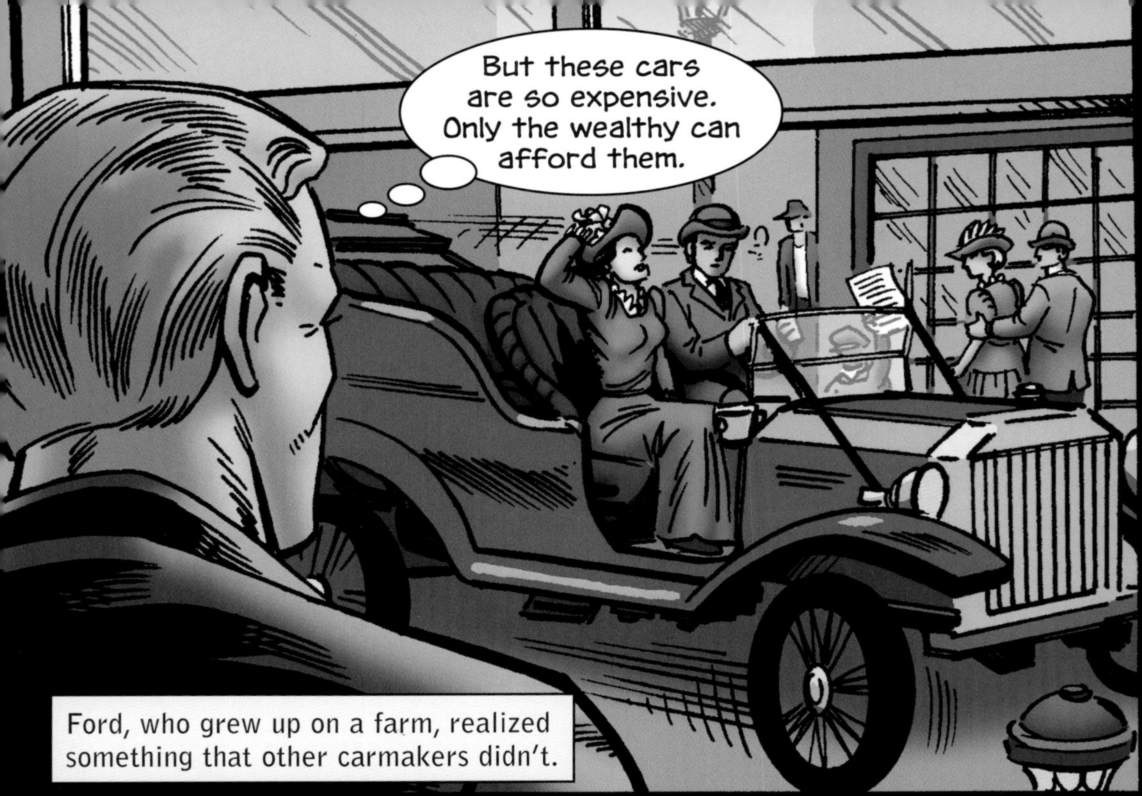
But these cars are so expensive. Only the wealthy can afford them.
Ford, who grew up on a farm, realized something that other carmakers didn't.

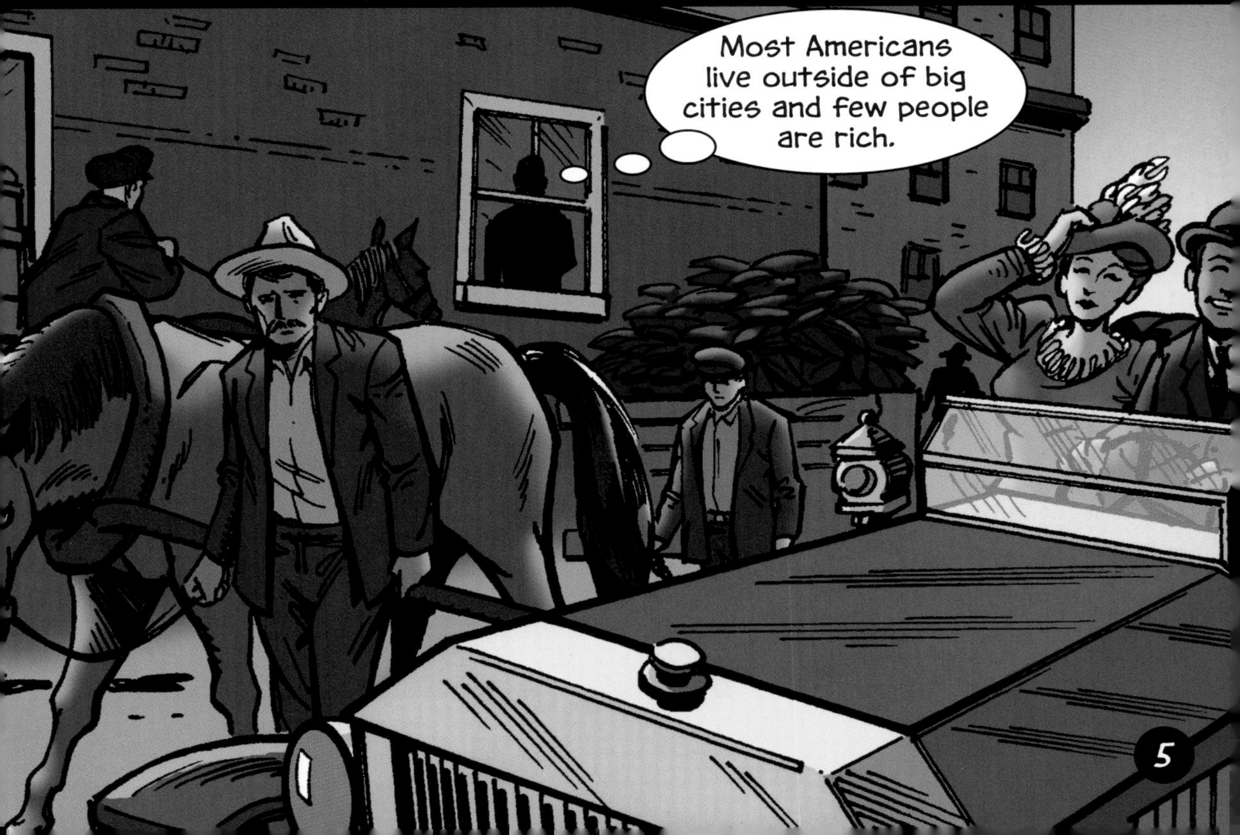
Most Americans live outside of big cities and few people are rich.

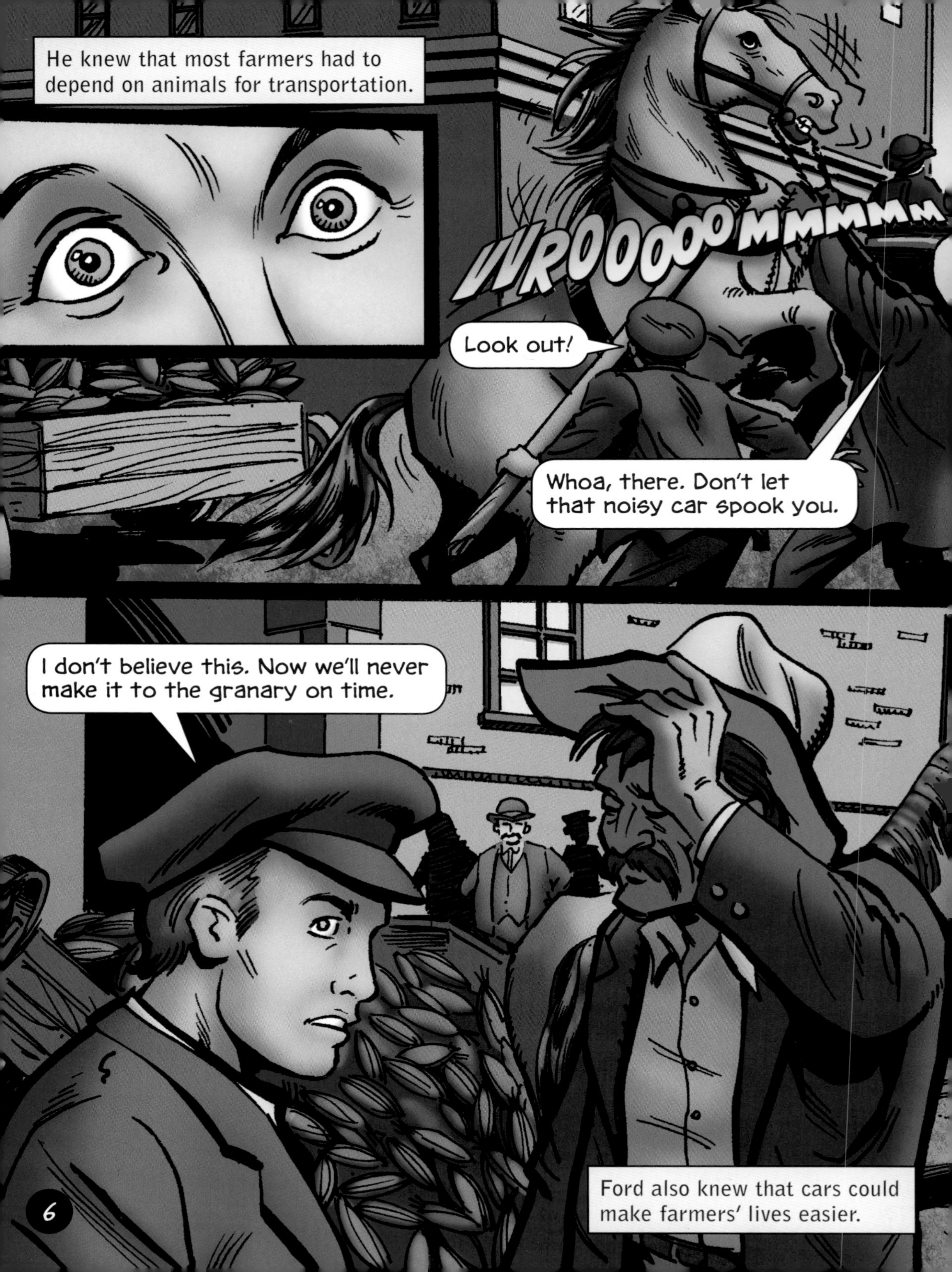
He knew that most farmers had to depend on animals for transportation.
VVROOOOOOMMMMMM
Look out!
Whoa, there. Don't let that noisy car spook you.
I don't believe this. Now we'll never make it to the granary on time.
Ford also knew that cars could make farmers' lives easier.

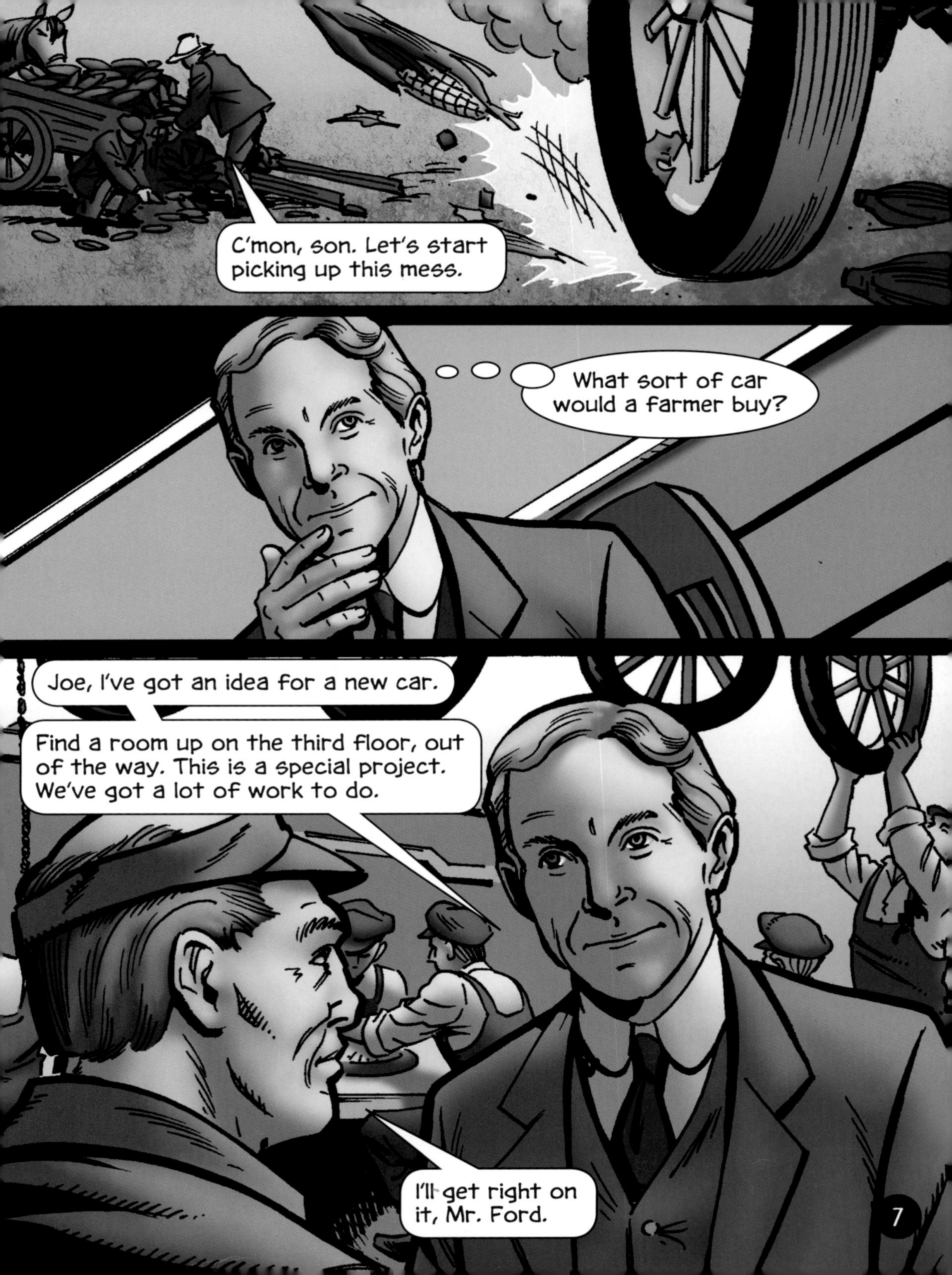

C'mon, son. Let's start picking up this mess.
What sort of car would a farmer buy?
Joe, I've got an idea for a new car.
Find a room up on the third floor, out of the way. This is a special project. We've got a lot of work to do.
I'll get right on it, Mr. Ford.

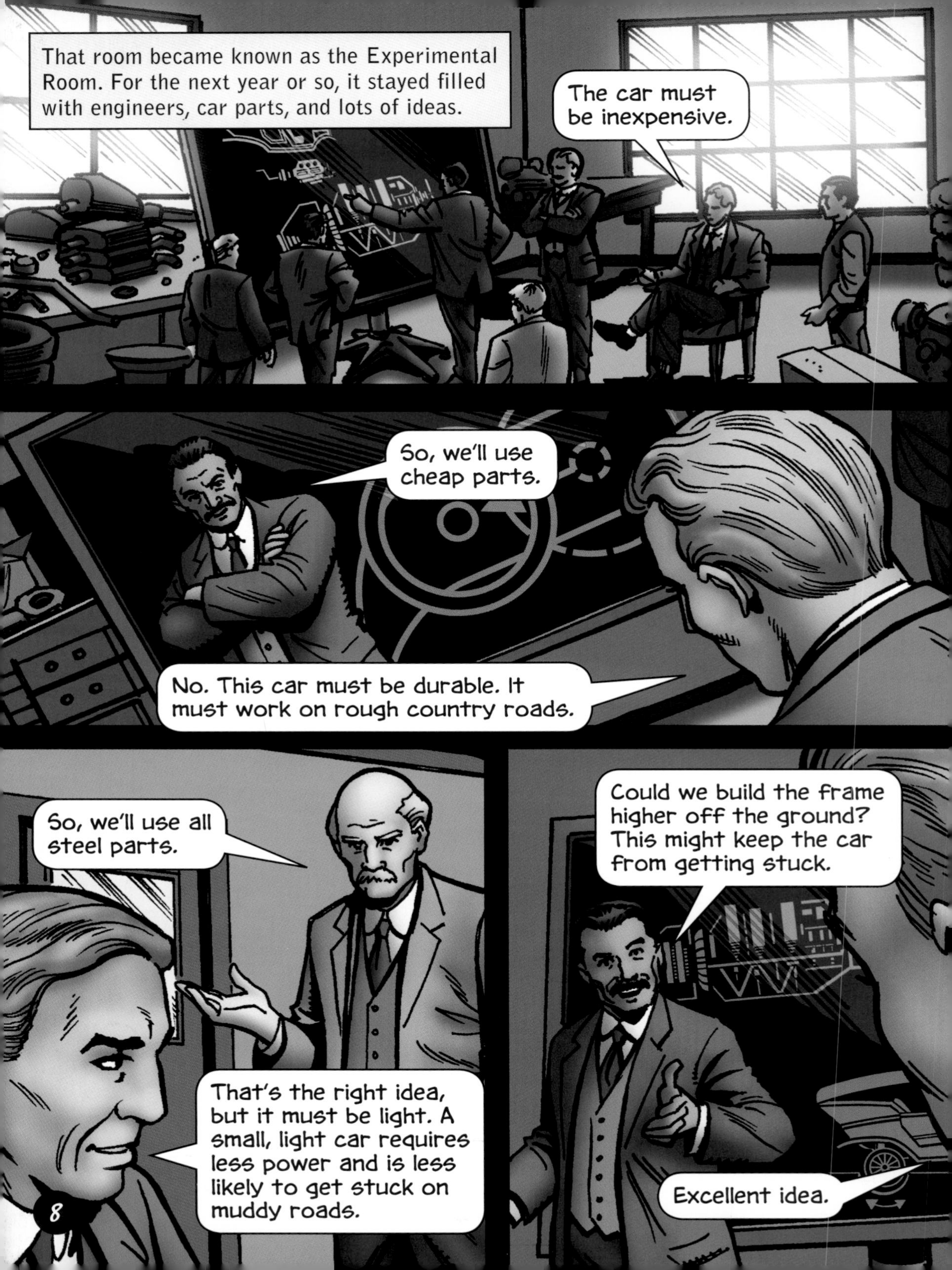
That room became known as the Experimental Room. For the next year or so, it stayed filled with engineers, car parts, and lots of ideas.
The car must be inexpensive.
So, we'll use cheap parts.
No. This car must be durable. It must work on rough country roads.
So, we'll use all steel parts.
That's the right idea, but it must be light. A small, light car requires less power and is less likely to get stuck on muddy roads.
Could we build the frame higher off the ground? This might keep the car from getting stuck.
Excellent idea.

Ford and his team developed a number of ideas for his new Model T car. They decided to build as many parts as possible from vanadium steel. This new type of steel was stronger and lighter than regular steel.

They also developed a one-piece cylinder block for the engine. Other engine blocks at the time were made of eight or more pieces and broke apart after hard use.

The gear system for the Model T allowed drivers to shift smoothly and quickly from forward to reverse. The car could be rocked back and forth to get out of ditches and potholes.

The steering wheel was moved from the center to the left. This change gave the driver a better view of oncoming traffic. It also allowed room for more people in the front seat.

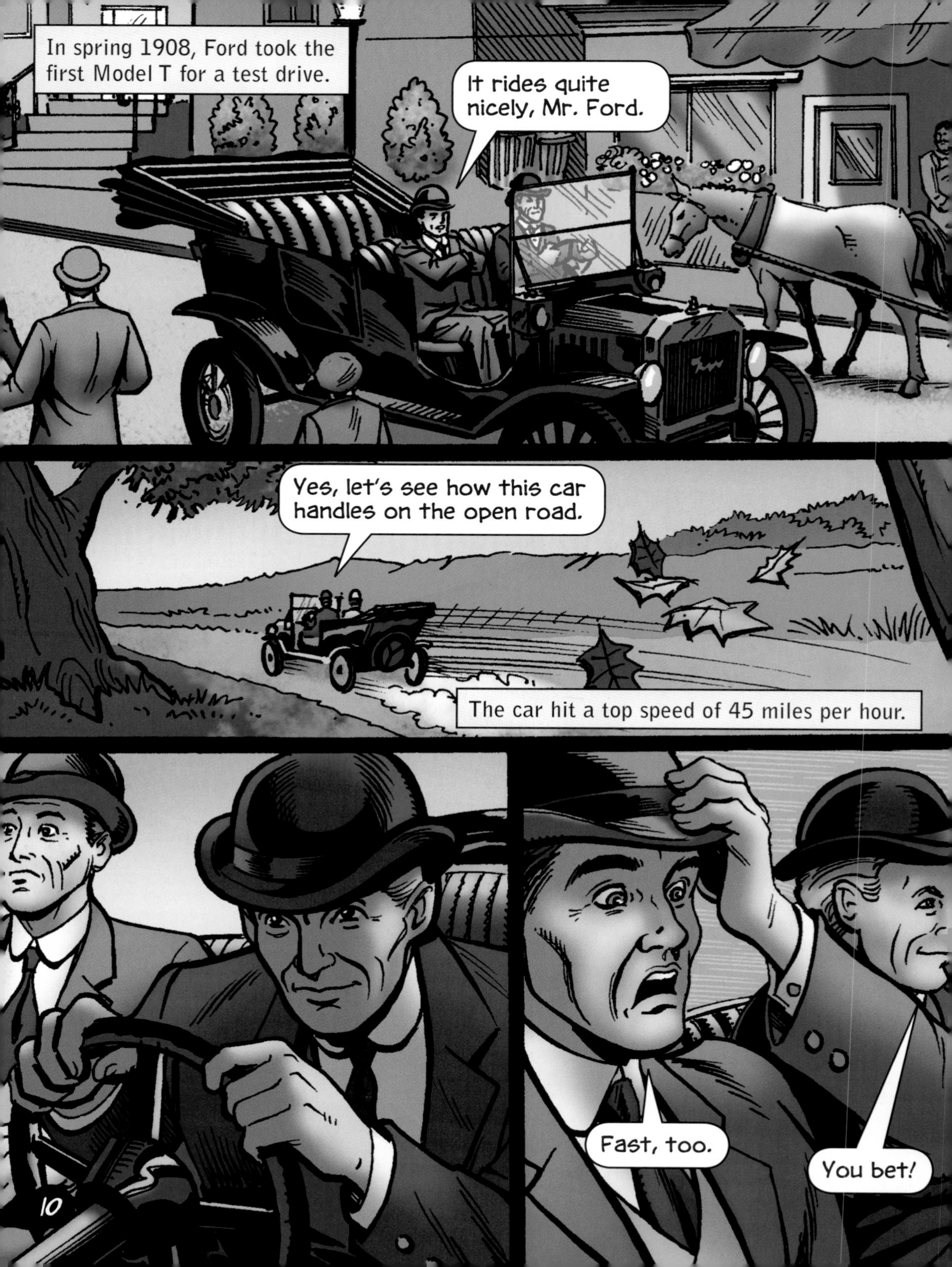
In spring 1908, Ford took the first Model T for a test drive.
It rides quite nicely, Mr. Ford.
Yes, let's see how this car handles on the open road.
The car hit a top speed of 45 miles per hour.
Fast, too.
You bet!

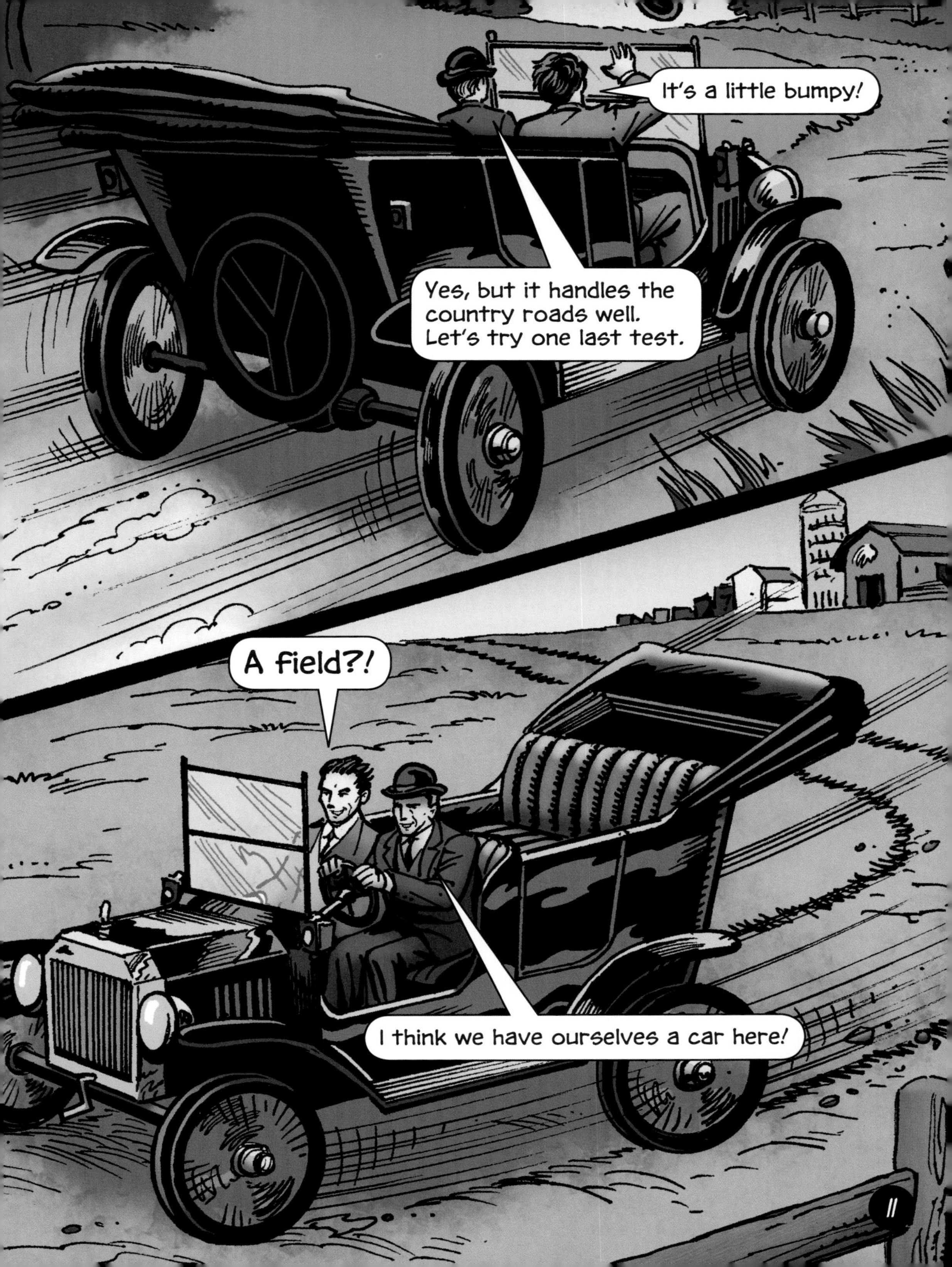
It's a little bumpy!
Yes, but it handles the country roads well. Let's try one last test.
A field?!
I think we have ourselves a car here!

SELLING THE MODEL T

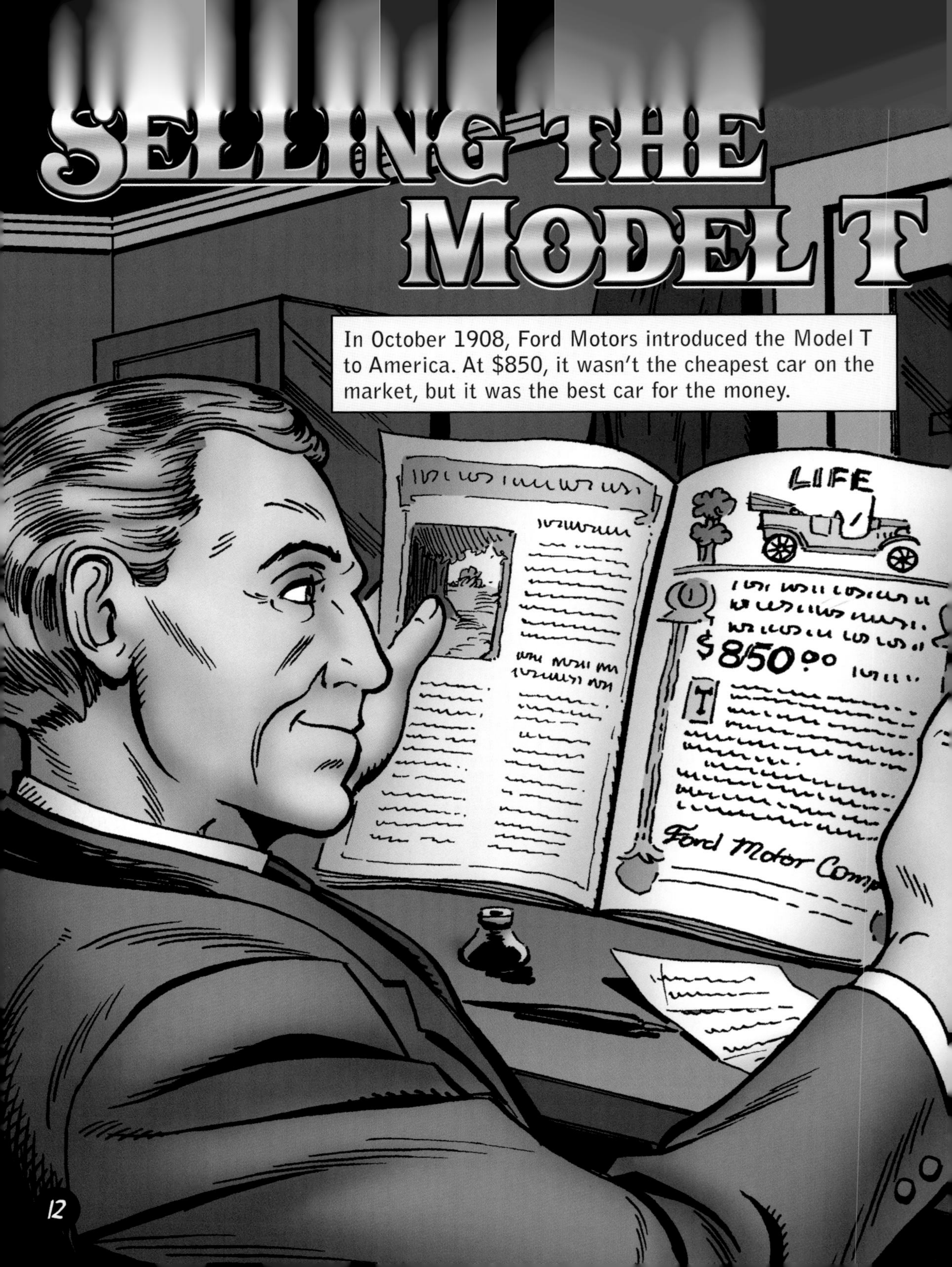
In October 1908, Ford Motors introduced the Model T to America. At $850, it wasn't the cheapest car on the market, but it was the best car for the money.
LIFE
$850.00
T
Ford Motor Comp

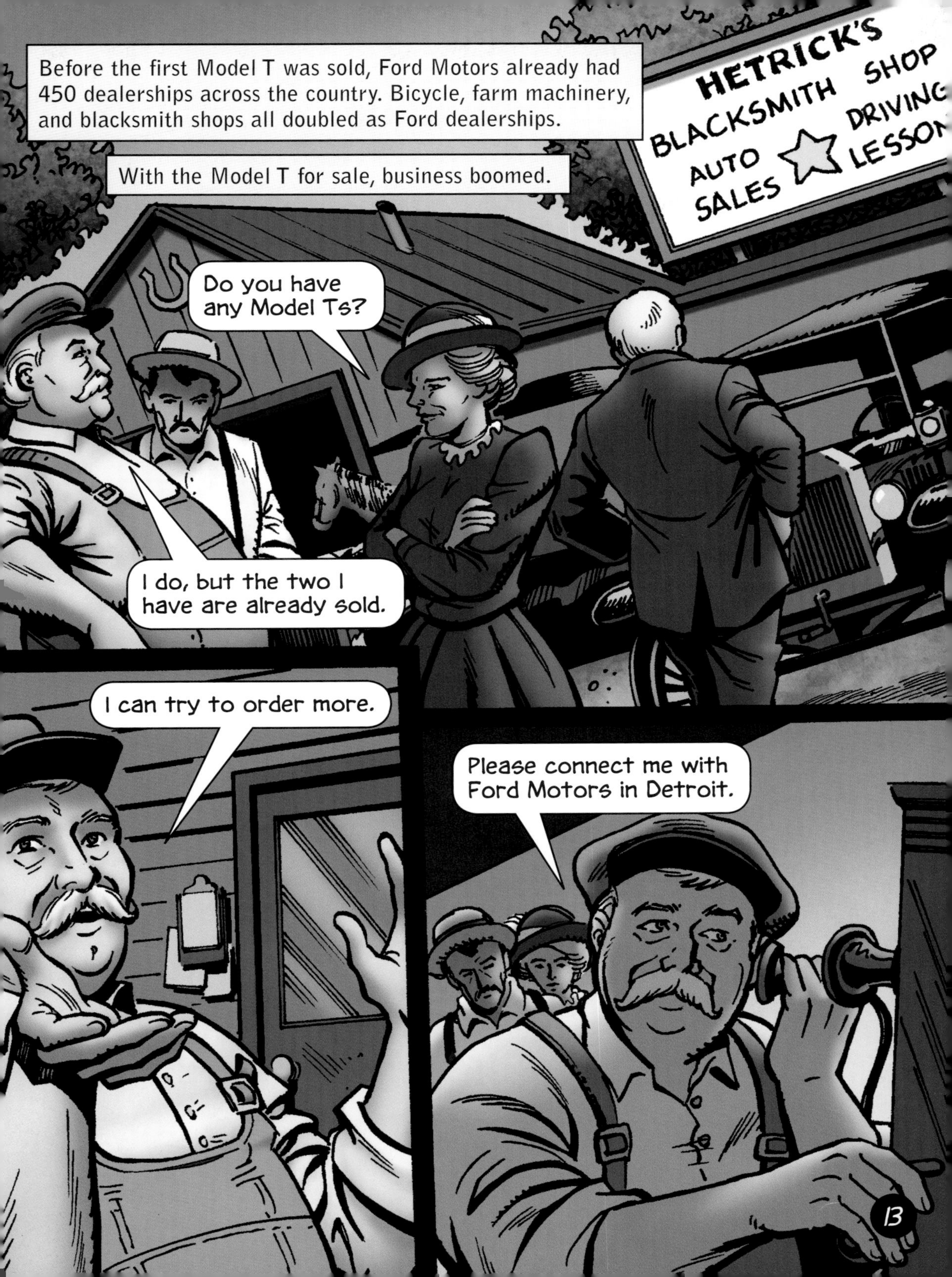

Before the first Model T was sold, Ford Motors already had 450 dealerships across the country. Bicycle, farm machinery, and blacksmith shops all doubled as Ford dealerships.
With the Model T for sale, business boomed.
HETRICK'S
BLACKSMITH SHOP
AUTO SALES
DRIVING LESSON
Do you have any Model Ts?
I do, but the two I have are already sold.
I can try to order more.
Please connect me with Ford Motors in Detroit.

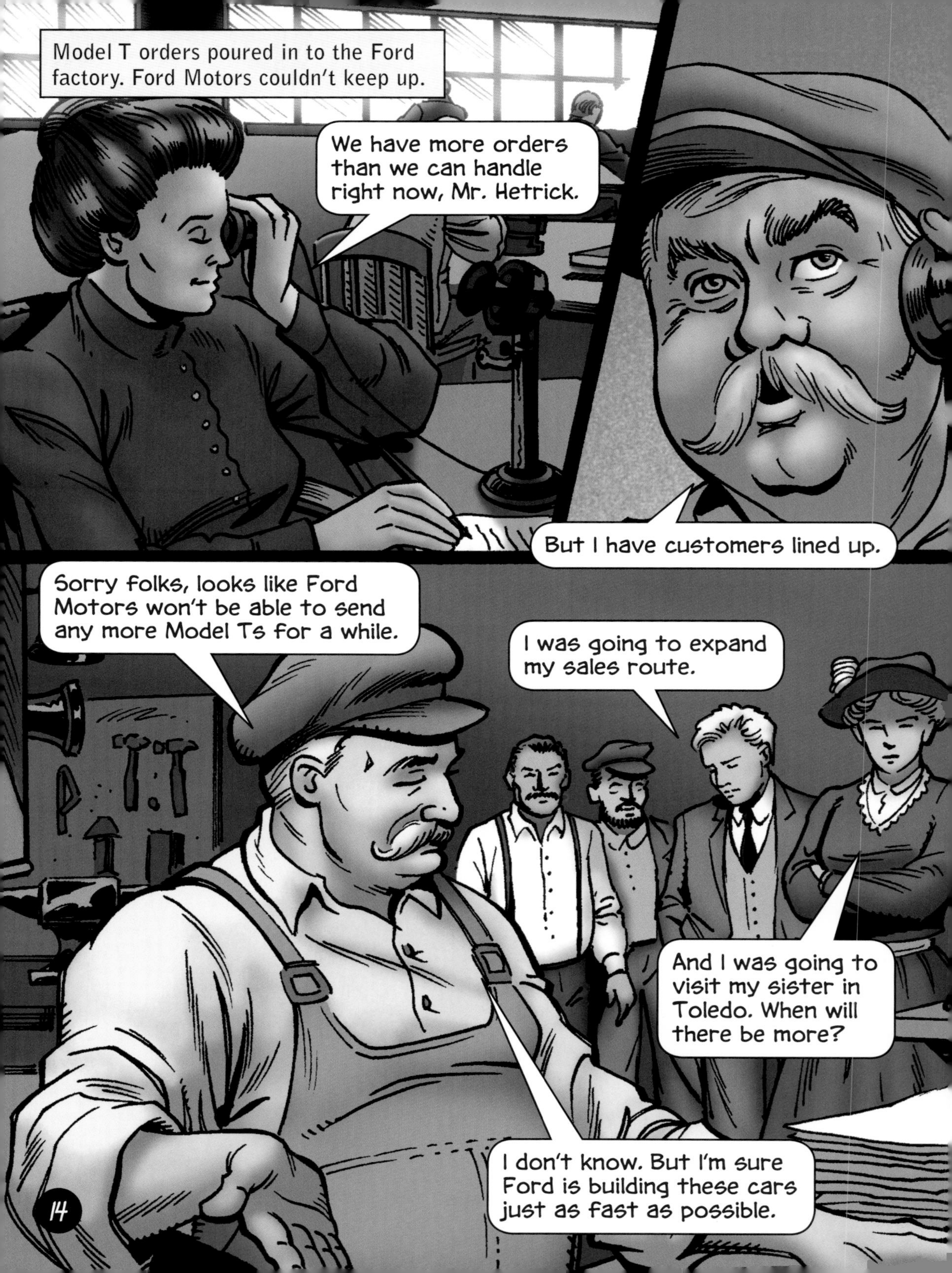
Model T orders poured in to the Ford factory. Ford Motors couldn't keep up.
We have more orders than we can handle right now, Mr. Hetrick.
But I have customers lined up.
Sorry folks, looks like Ford Motors won't be able to send any more Model Ts for a while.
I was going to expand my sales route.
And I was going to visit my sister in Toledo. When will there be more?
I don't know. But I'm sure Ford is building these cars just as fast as possible.

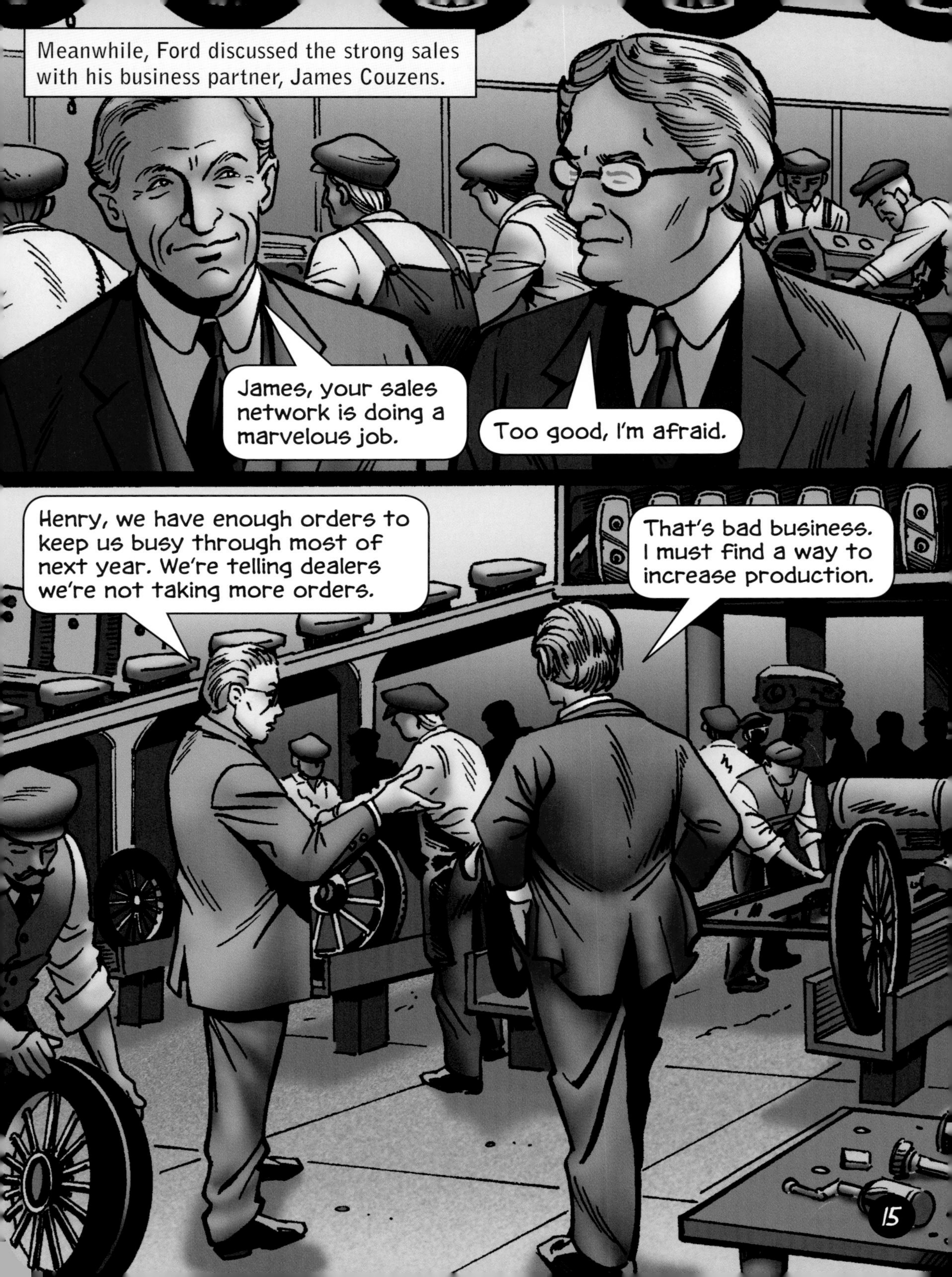
Meanwhile, Ford discussed the strong sales with his business partner, James Couzens.
James, your sales network is doing a marvelous job.
Too good, I'm afraid.
Henry, we have enough orders to keep us busy through most of next year. We're telling dealers we're not taking more orders.
That's bad business. I must find a way to increase production.

CHAPTER 3

15 MILLION MODEL Ts

In 1910, Ford opened the largest auto factory in the world at Highland Park in Detroit. It was 865 feet long and four stories tall.

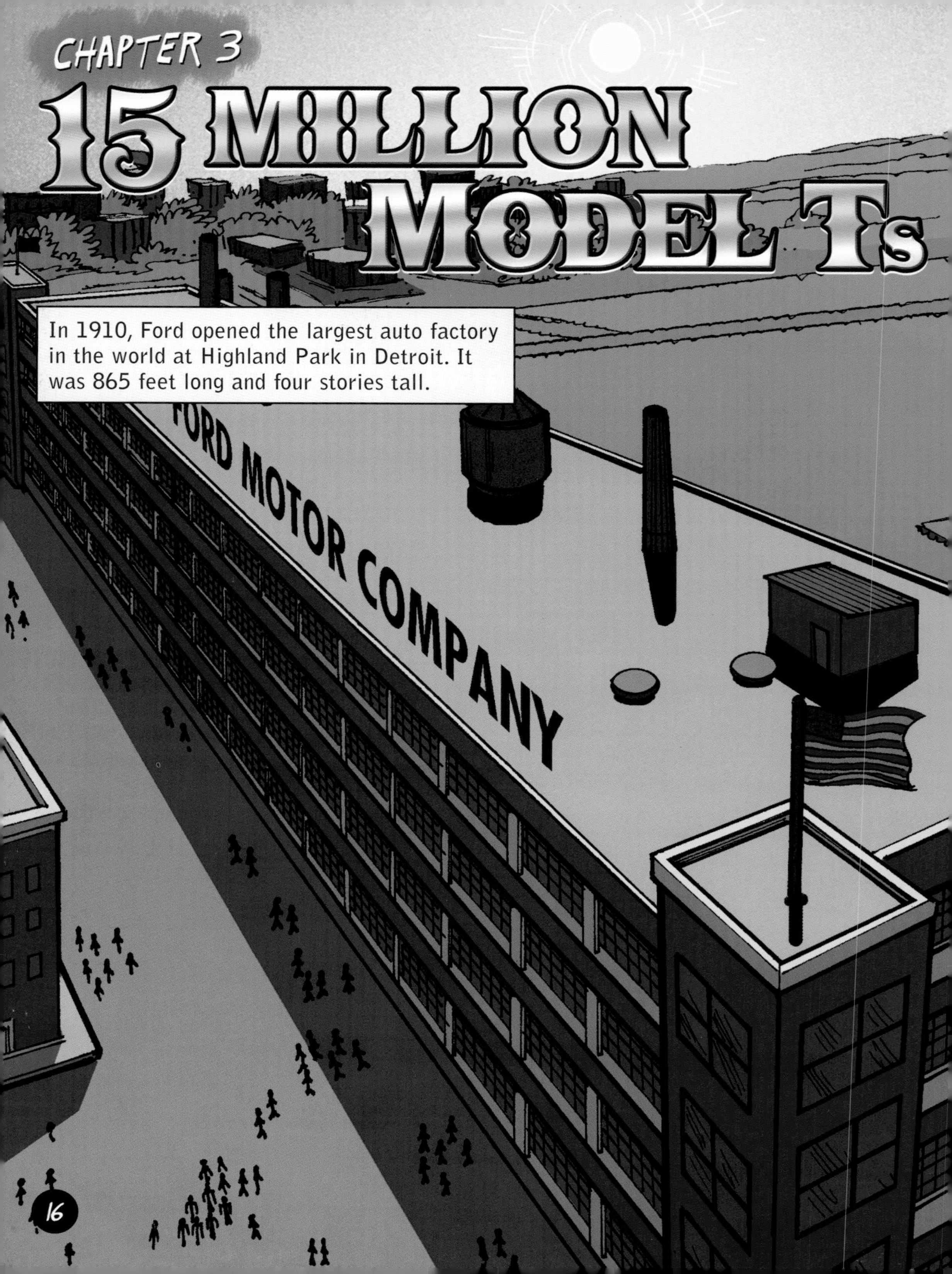

FORD MOTOR COMPANY

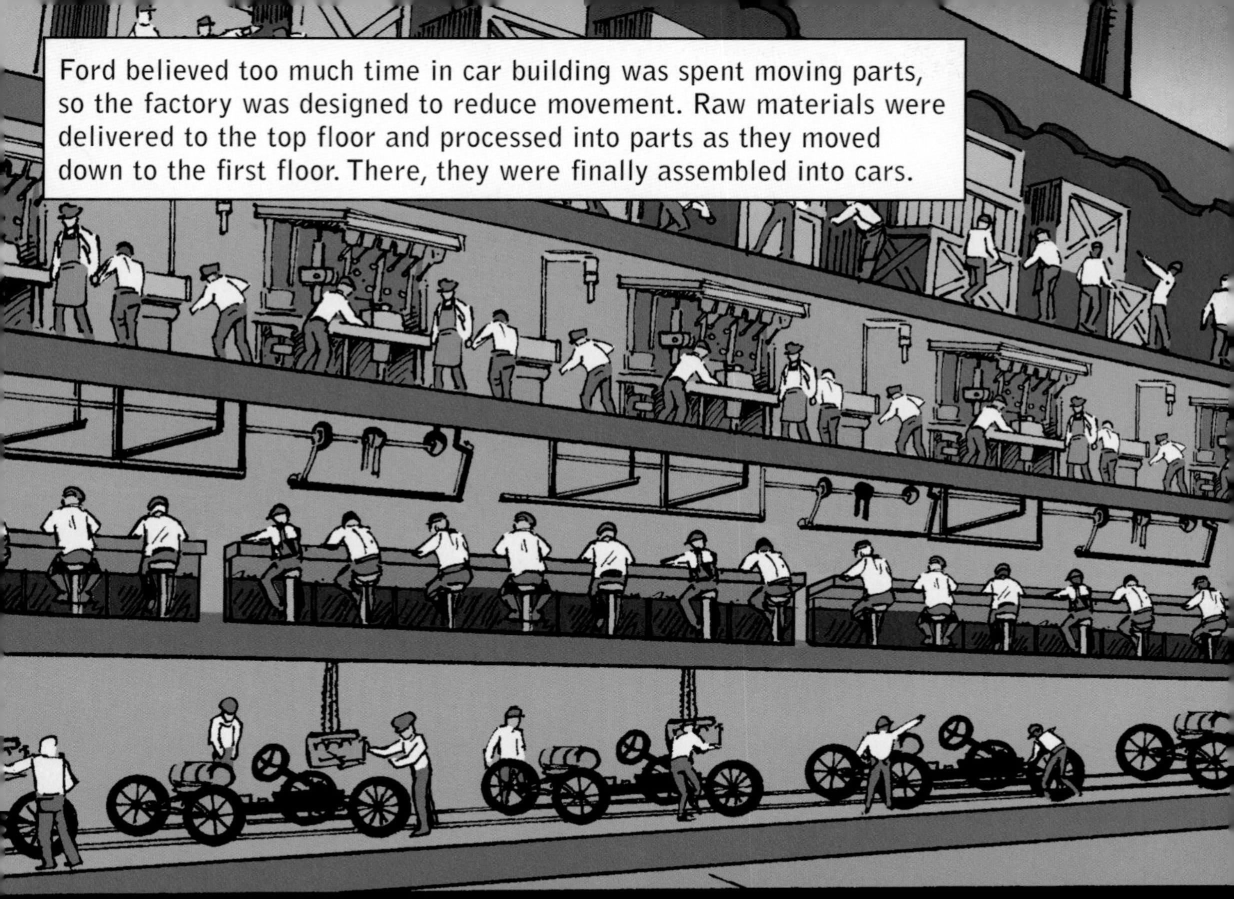
Ford believed too much time in car building was spent moving parts, so the factory was designed to reduce movement. Raw materials were delivered to the top floor and processed into parts as they moved down to the first floor. There, they were finally assembled into cars.

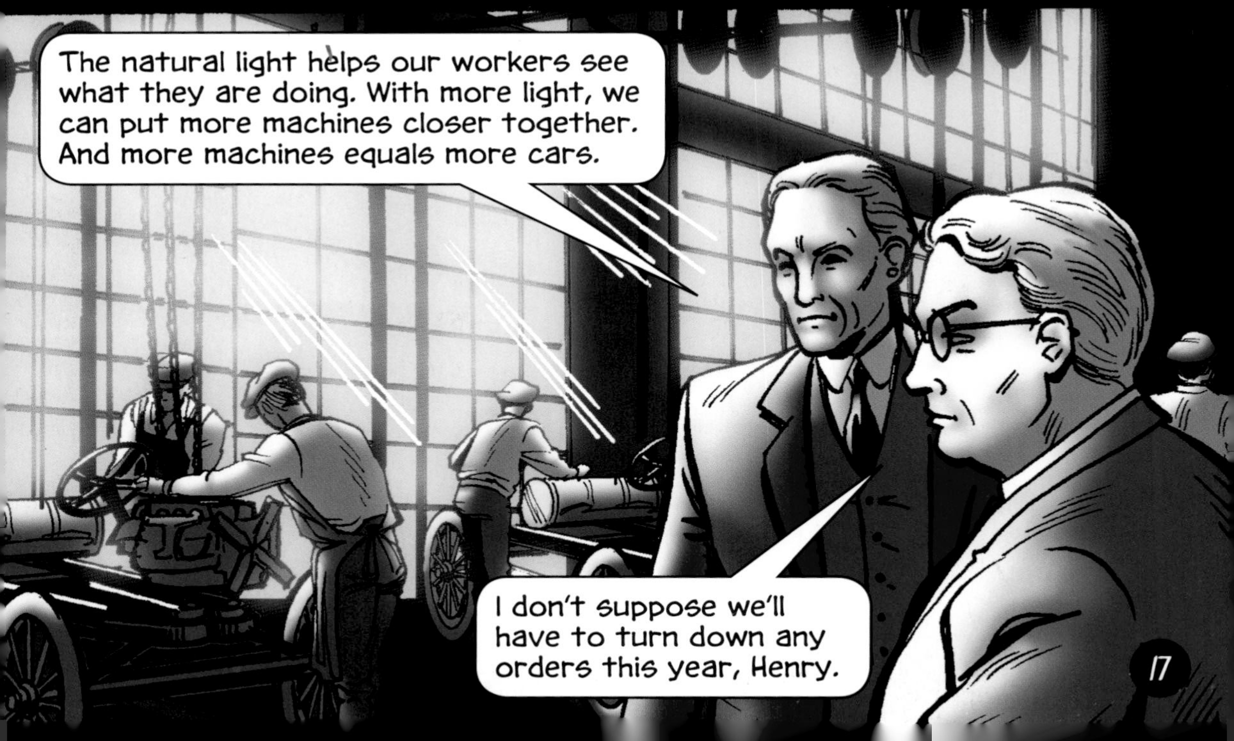
The natural light helps our workers see what they are doing. With more light, we can put more machines closer together. And more machines equals more cars.
I don't suppose we'll have to turn down any orders this year, Henry.

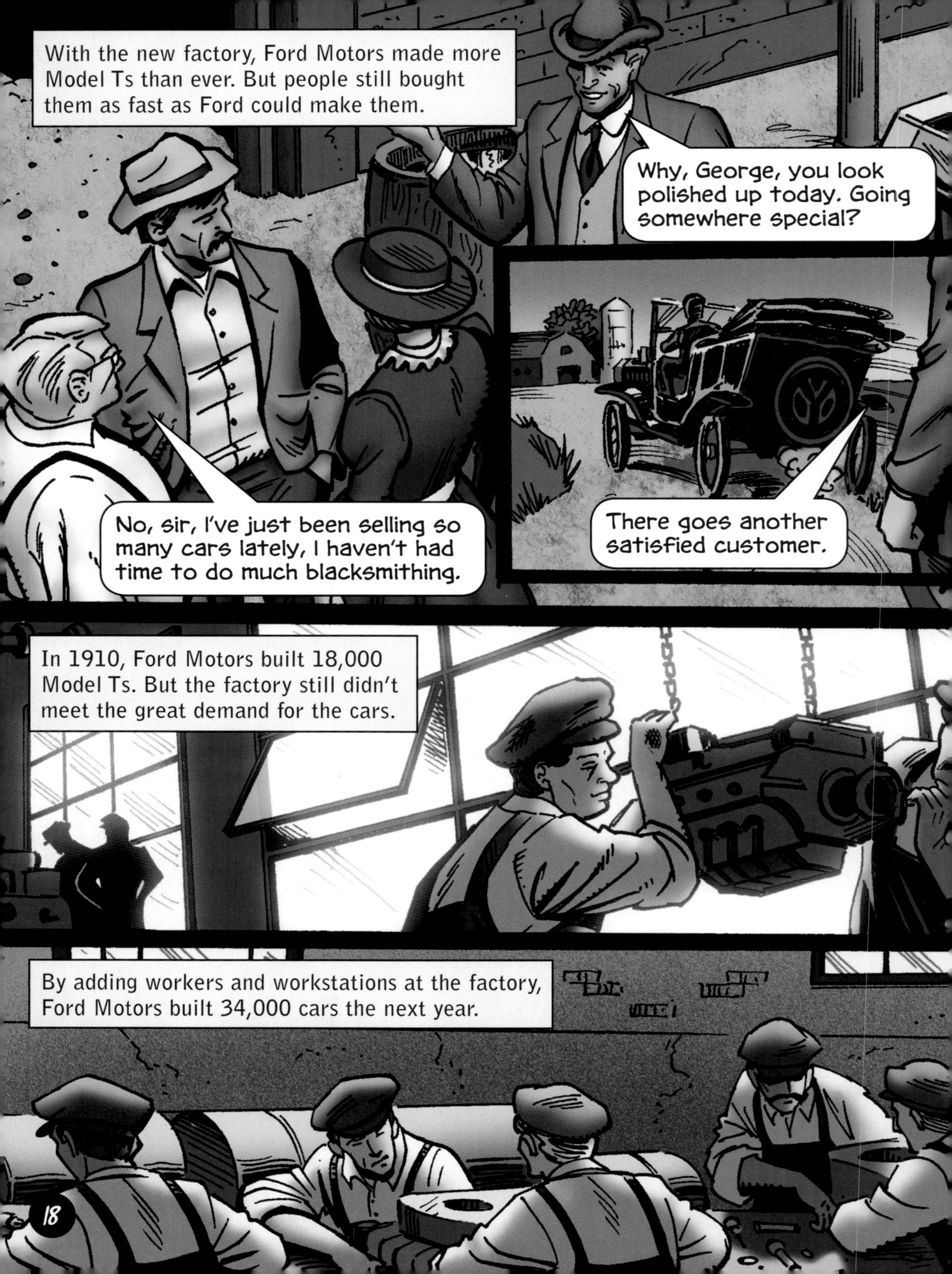
With the new factory, Ford Motors made more Model Ts than ever. But people still bought them as fast as Ford could make them.
Why, George, you look polished up today. Going somewhere special?
No, sir, I've just been selling so many cars lately, I haven't had time to do much blacksmithing.
There goes another satisfied customer.
In 1910, Ford Motors built 18,000 Model Ts. But the factory still didn't meet the great demand for the cars.
By adding workers and workstations at the factory, Ford Motors built 34,000 cars the next year.

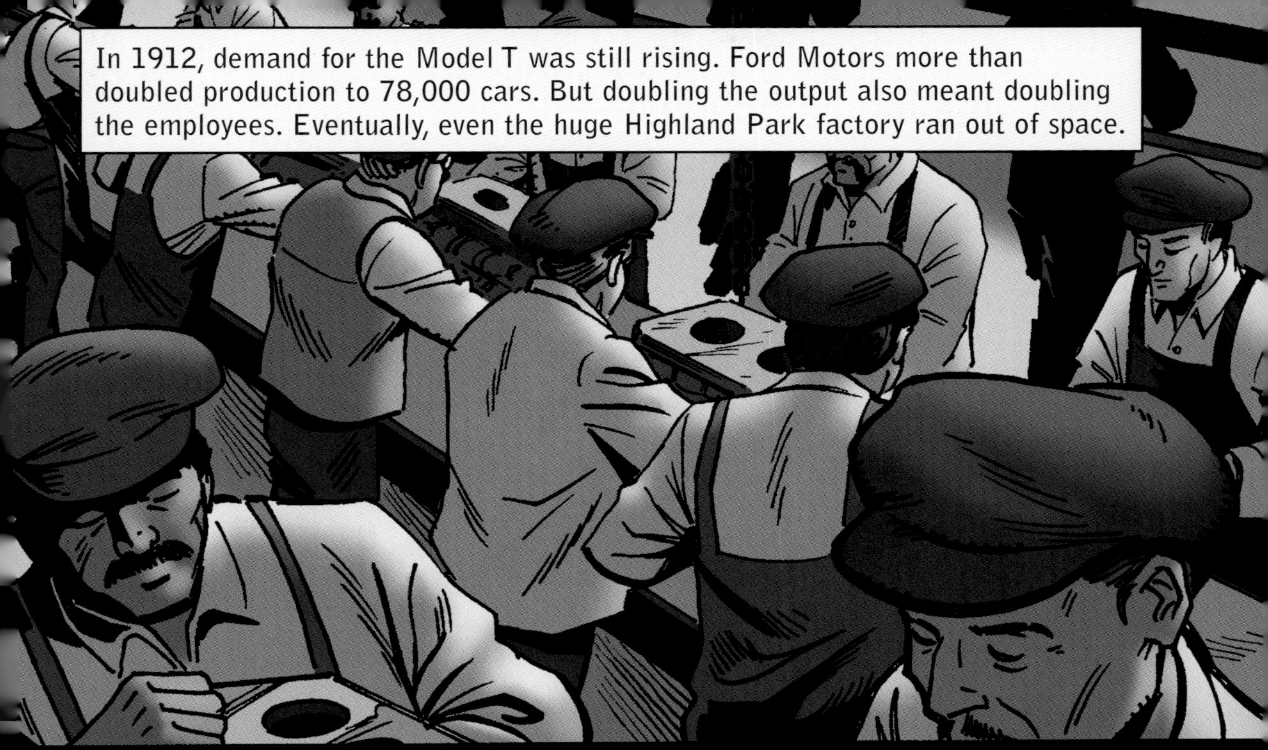
In 1912, demand for the Model T was still rising. Ford Motors more than doubled production to 78,000 cars. But doubling the output also meant doubling the employees. Eventually, even the huge Highland Park factory ran out of space.

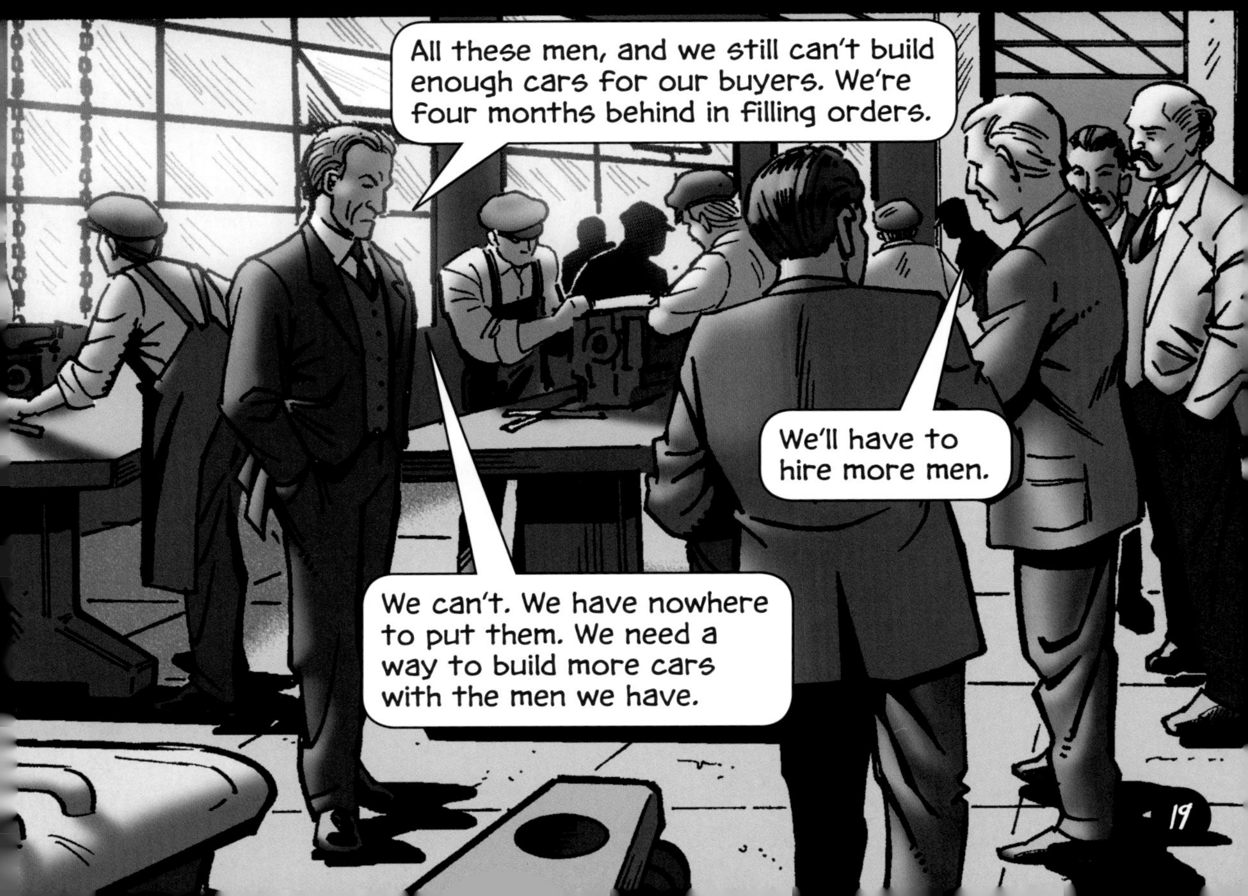
All these men, and we still can't build enough cars for our buyers. We're four months behind in filling orders.
We'll have to hire more men.
We can't. We have nowhere to put them. We need a way to build more cars with the men we have.

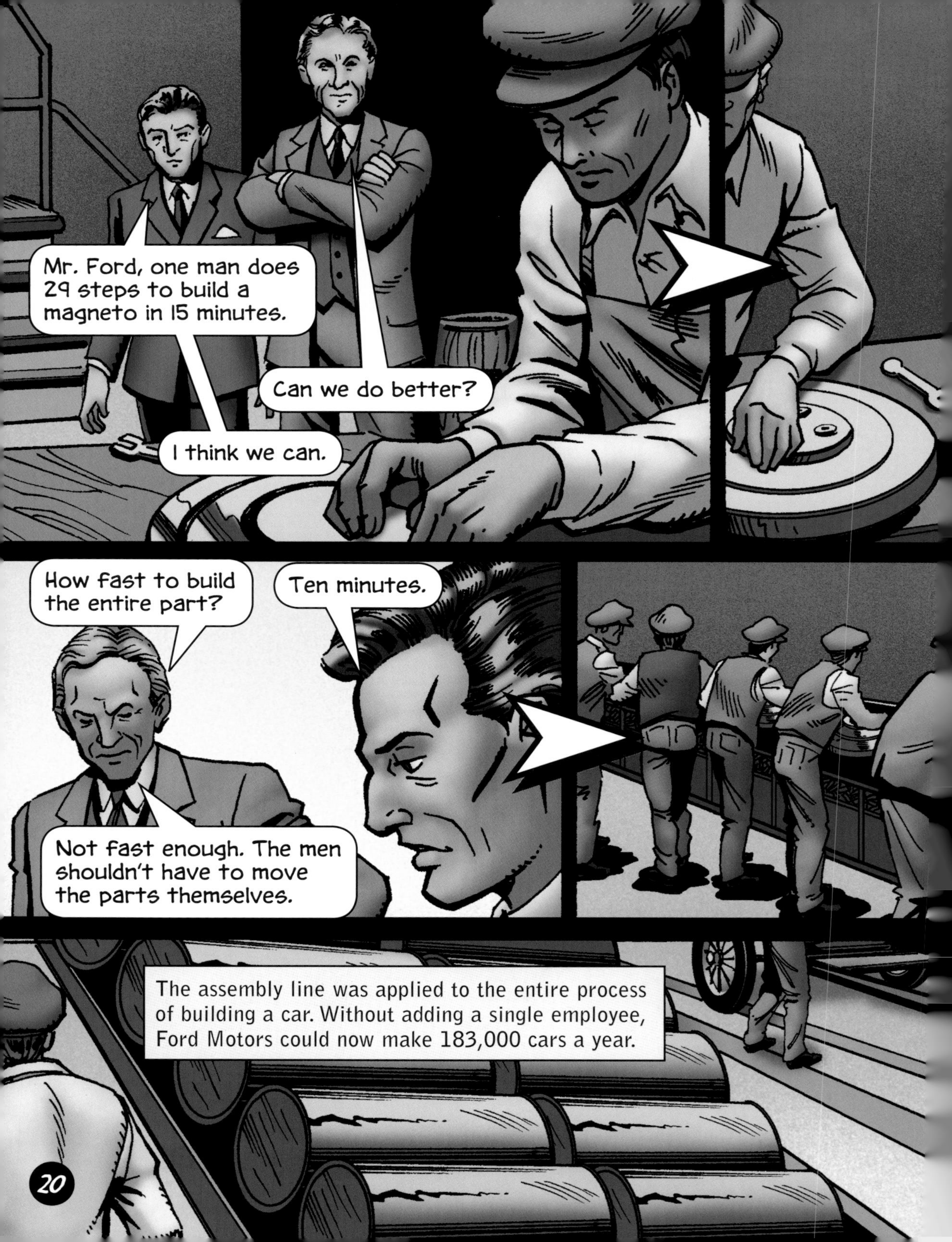

Mr. Ford, one man does 29 steps to build a magneto in 15 minutes.
Can we do better?
I think we can.
How fast to build the entire part?
Ten minutes.
Not fast enough. The men shouldn't have to move the parts themselves.
The assembly line was applied to the entire process of building a car. Without adding a single employee, Ford Motors could now make 183,000 cars a year.

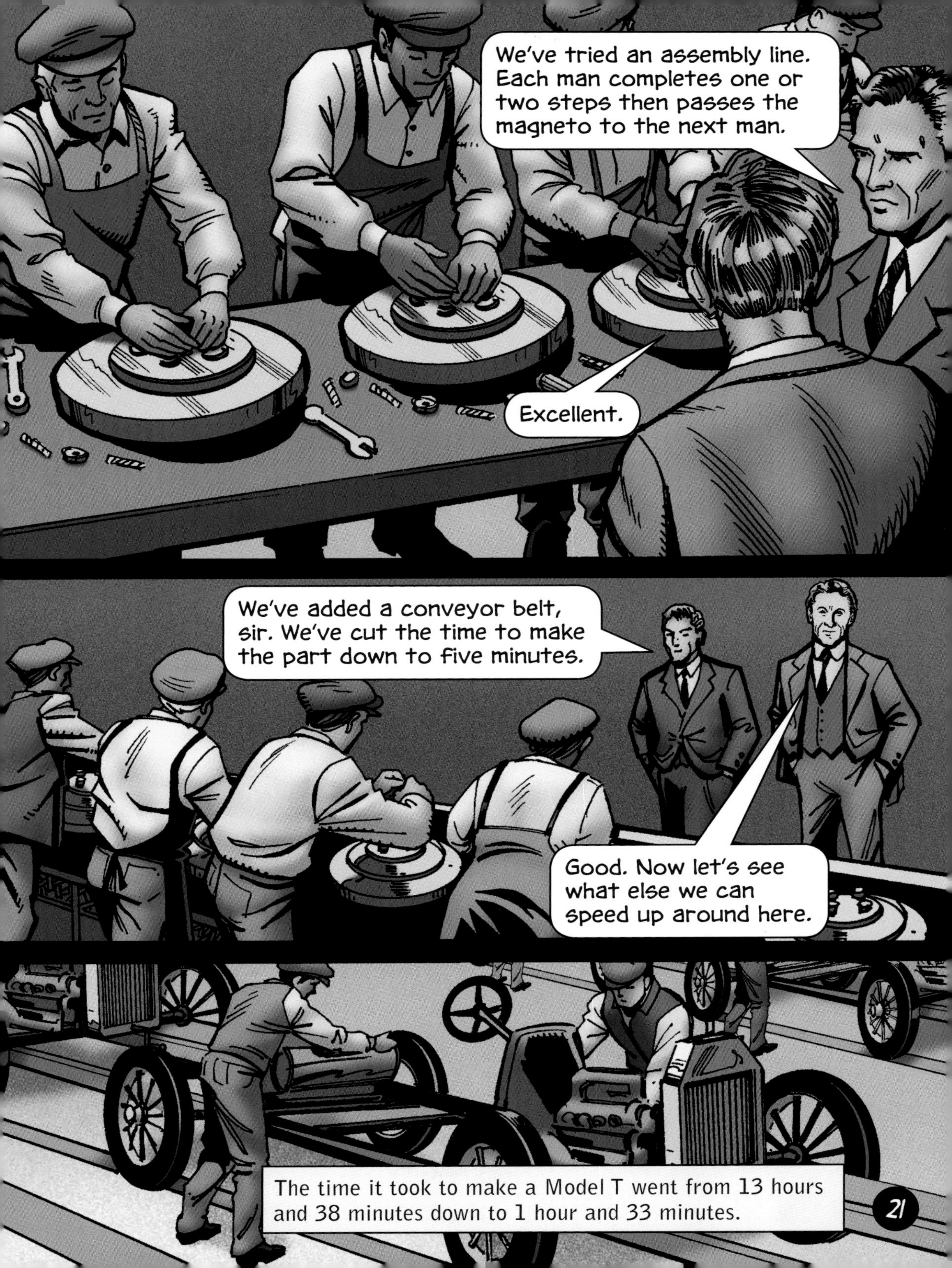
We've tried an assembly line. Each man completes one or two steps then passes the magneto to the next man.
Excellent.
We've added a conveyor belt, sir. We've cut the time to make the part down to five minutes.
Good. Now let's see what else we can speed up around here.

The time it took to make a Model T went from 13 hours and 38 minutes down to 1 hour and 33 minutes.

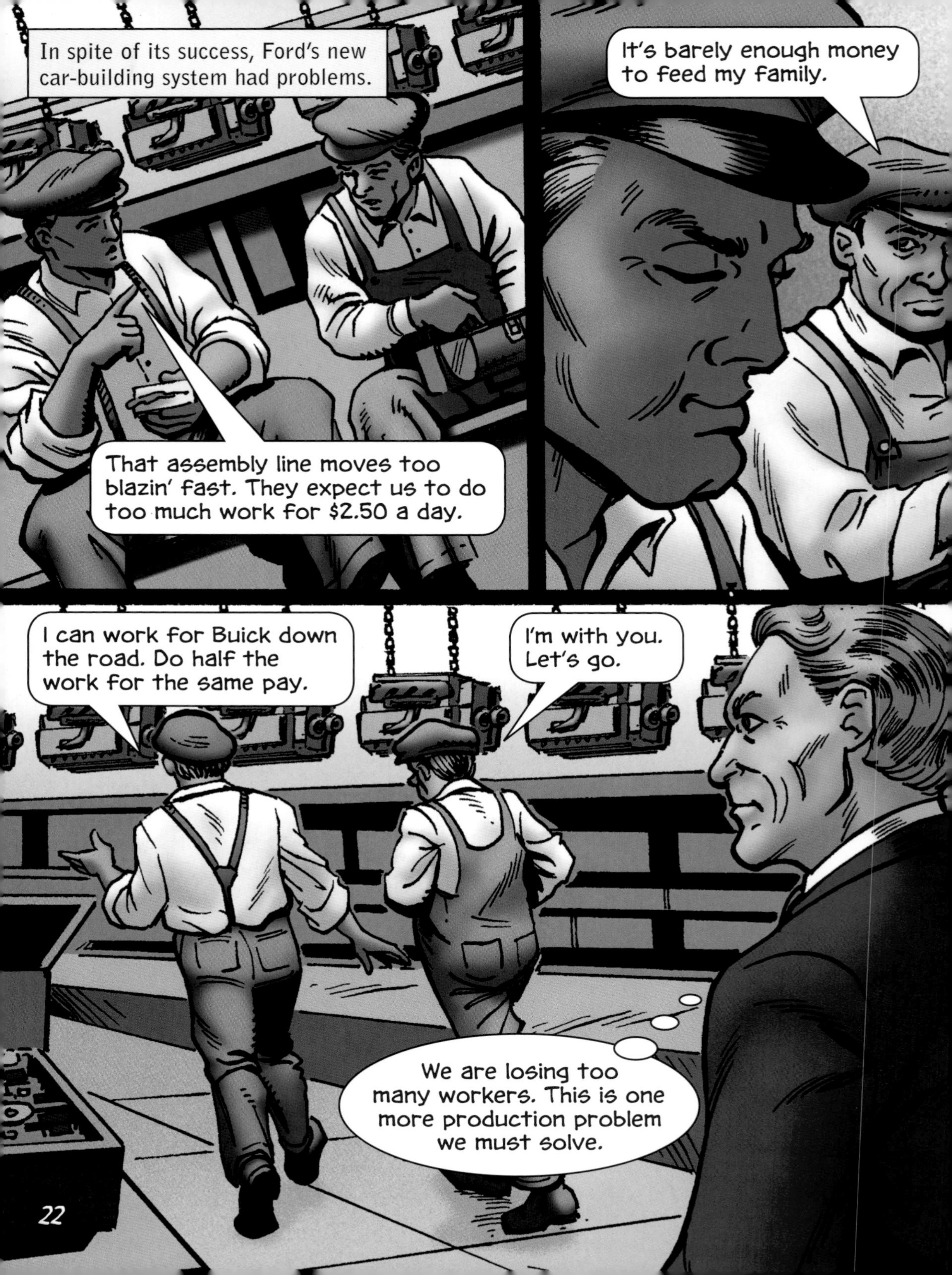

In spite of its success, Ford's new car-building system had problems.
That assembly line moves too blazin' fast. They expect us to do too much work for $2.50 a day.
It's barely enough money to feed my family.
I can work for Buick down the road. Do half the work for the same pay.
I'm with you. Let's go.
We are losing too many workers. This is one more production problem we must solve.

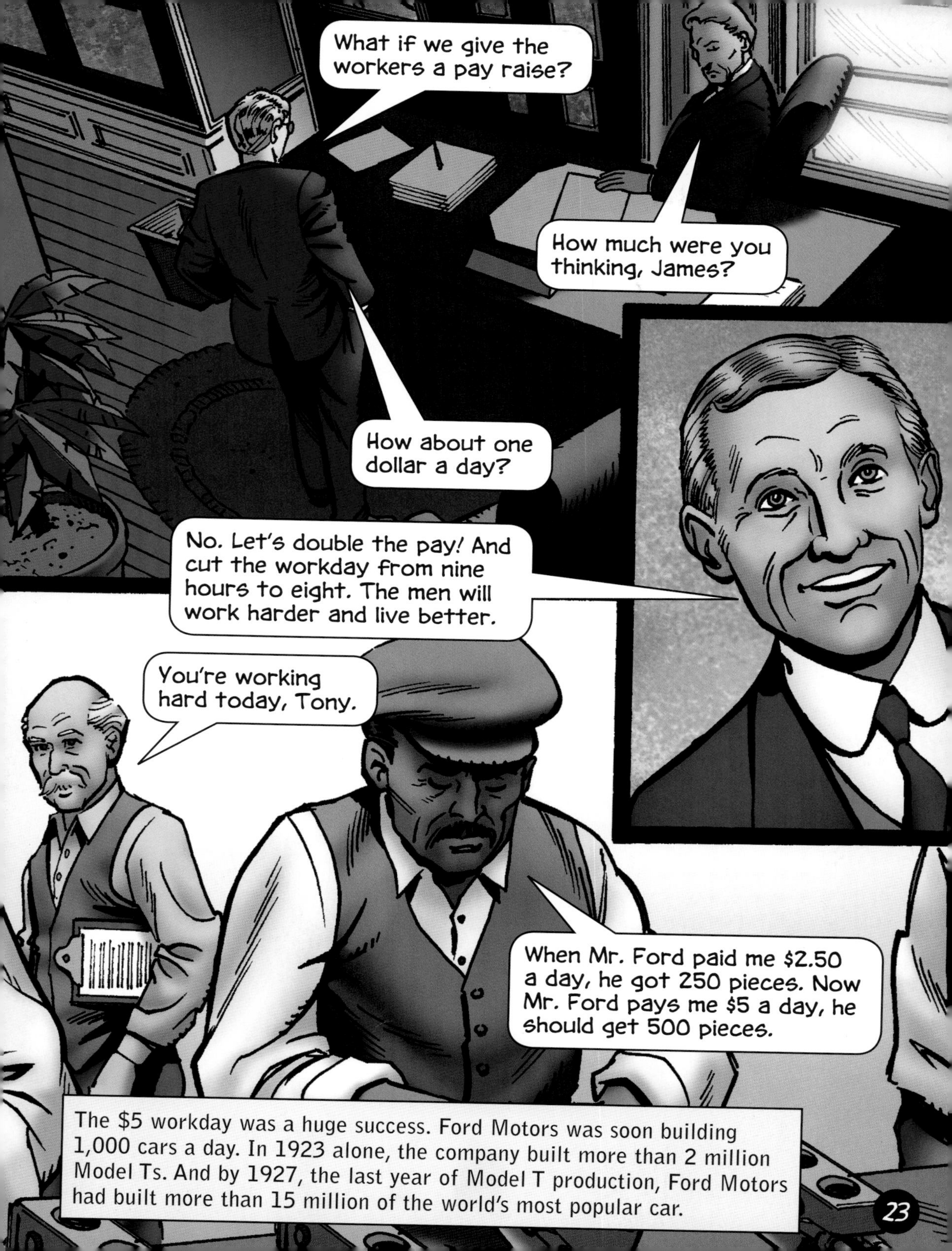
What if we give the workers a pay raise?
How much were you thinking, James?
How about one dollar a day?
No. Let's double the pay! And cut the workday from nine hours to eight. The men will work harder and live better.
You're working hard today, Tony.
When Mr. Ford paid me $2.50 a day, he got 250 pieces. Now Mr. Ford pays me $5 a day, he should get 500 pieces.
The $5 workday was a huge success. Ford Motors was soon building 1,000 cars a day. In 1923 alone, the company built more than 2 million Model Ts. And by 1927, the last year of Model T production, Ford Motors had built more than 15 million of the world's most popular car.

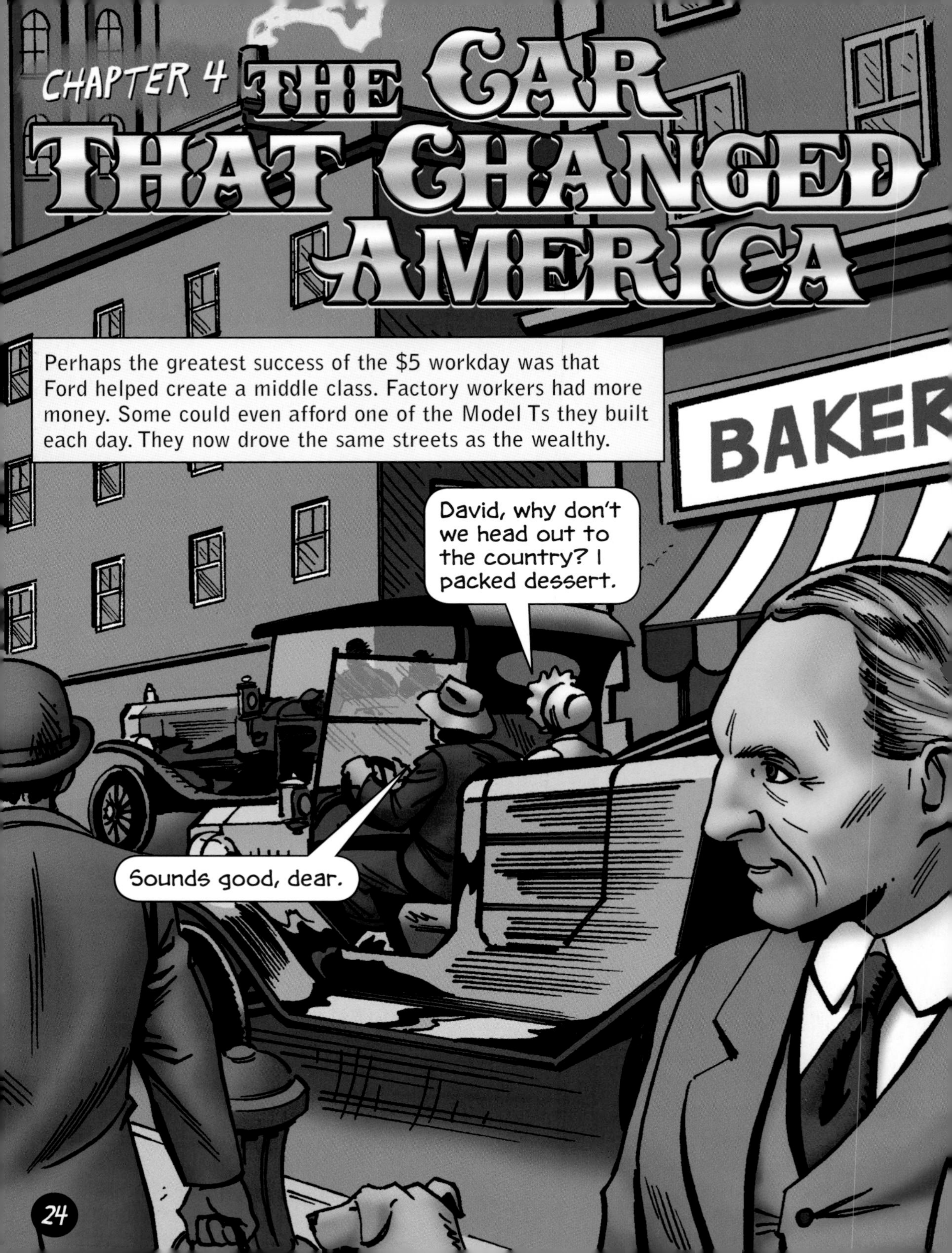
CHAPTER 4 THE CAR THAT CHANGED AMERICA
Perhaps the greatest success of the $5 workday was that Ford helped create a middle class. Factory workers had more money. Some could even afford one of the Model Ts they built each day. They now drove the same streets as the wealthy.
BAKER
David, why don't we head out to the country? I packed dessert.
Sounds good, dear.

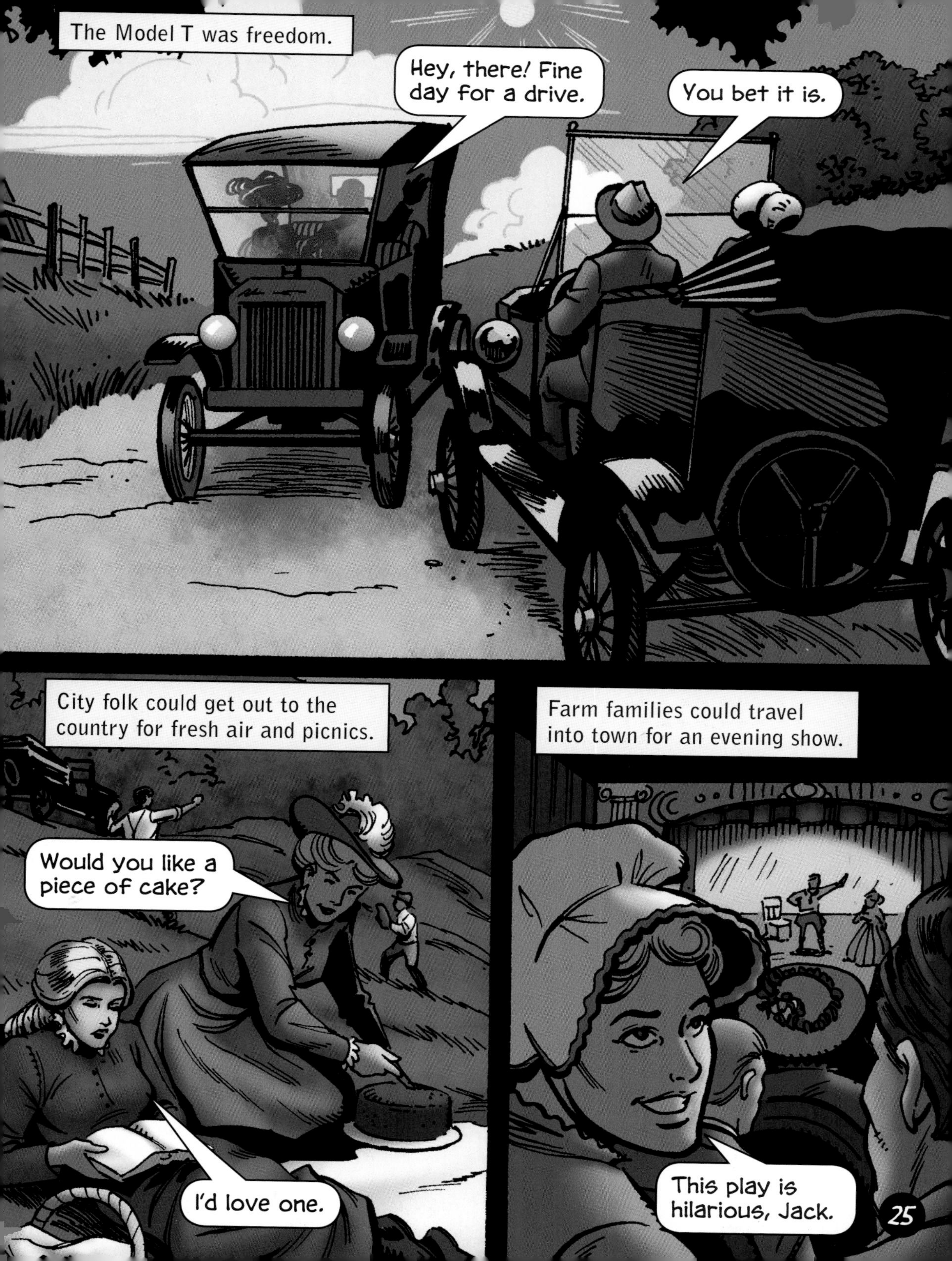
The Model T was freedom.
Hey, there! Fine day for a drive.
You bet it is.
City folk could get out to the country for fresh air and picnics.
Would you like a piece of cake?
I'd love one.
Farm families could travel into town for an evening show.
This play is hilarious, Jack.

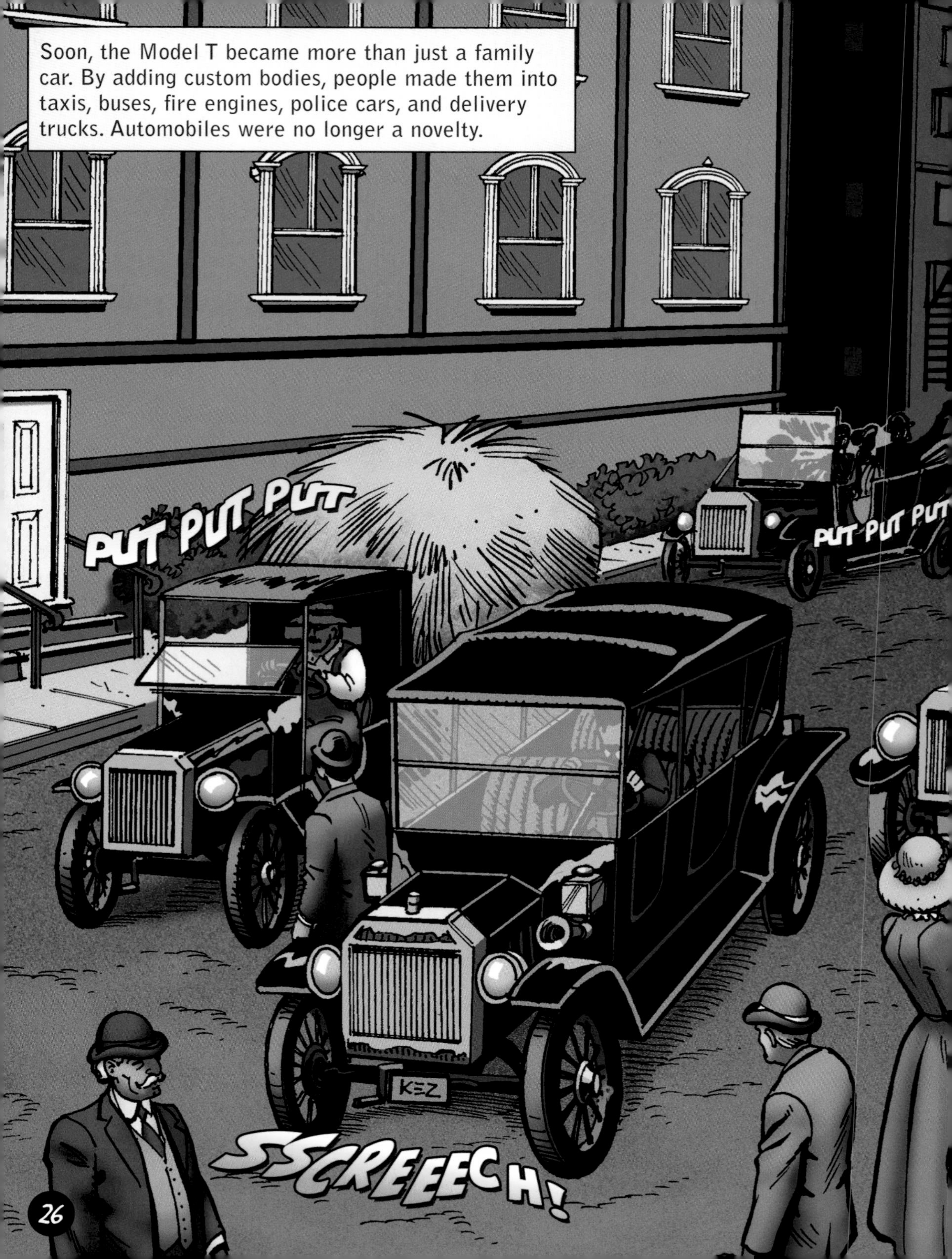
Soon, the Model T became more than just a family car. By adding custom bodies, people made them into taxis, buses, fire engines, police cars, and delivery trucks. Automobiles were no longer a novelty.
PUT PUT PUT
PUT PUT PUT
SSCREEECH!

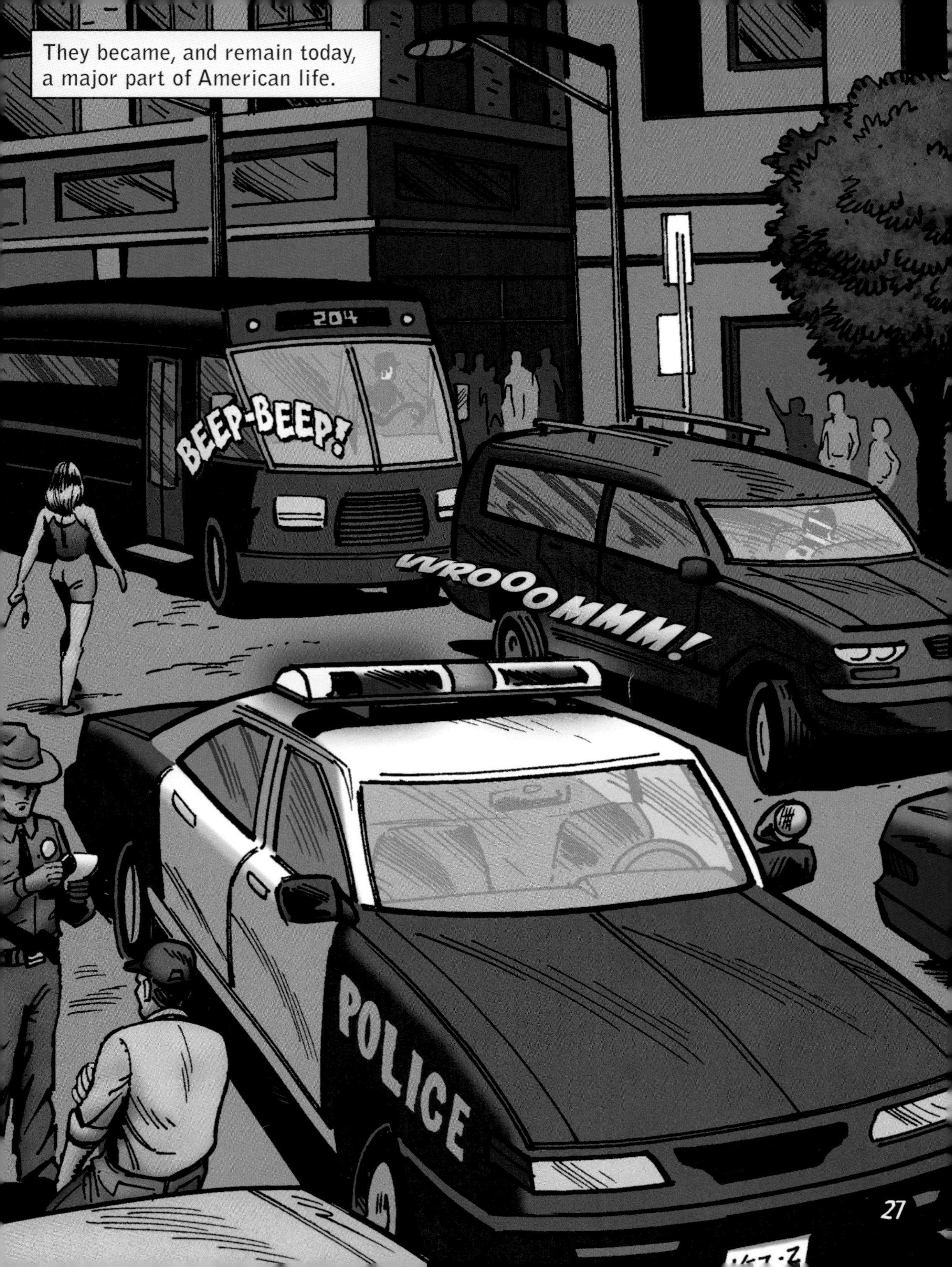
They became, and remain today, a major part of American life.
204
BEEP-BEEP!
VROOOOMMMM!
POLICE

MORE ABOUT
HENRY FORD AND THE MODEL T

Henry Ford was born in Greenfield, Michigan, on July 30, 1863. Ford married Clara Bryant in 1888. Their only child, Edsel, was born in 1893. Ford died on April 7, 1947, in Dearborn, Michigan. He was 83 years old.

On Christmas Eve 1893, Ford tested his first gasoline engine by clamping it to his kitchen sink. He connected a wire to the kitchen light socket to power the spark plug. Ford cranked the engine as his wife, Clara, dripped gasoline into the intake valve. As the engine rumbled to life, flames shot out the exhaust, filling the room with smoke and rattling the dishes and windows.

Ford built his first car, called the quadricycle, in a brick shed behind his Detroit home. When it was finished, he realized it was too wide to fit through the door. To get the car out for a test drive, Ford broke down one of the brick walls with an axe.

Early Model Ts were made in a variety of colors. But from 1914 to 1926, all Model Ts were painted black. The change was made because the black paint dried faster than the other paint colors. Fast-drying paint sped up the production of the car.

The Highland Park factory was nicknamed the Crystal Palace because the walls and ceilings held 50,000 square feet (4,645 square meters) of windows.

 The Model T was so popular that by 1918, half of the cars in the United States were Model Ts.

 The announcement of the $5 wage almost caused a riot at the Ford factory. Hundreds of workers from all over the country wanted to be hired. Ford made sure to hire black workers, disabled workers, and women, which was an unusual practice at the time.

 The Model T, like a favorite horse, was often thought of as part of the family. People often gave their Model T a name. Two popular nicknames were "Tin Lizzie" and "Flivver."

GLOSSARY

assembly line (uh-SEM-blee LINE)—an arrangement of machines and workers in a factory, where work passes from one person or machine to the next until the job is complete

blacksmith (BLAK-smith)—a person who makes and fixes things made of iron

engineer (en-juh-NIHR)—a person who is trained to design and build machines

magneto (mag-NET-oh)—an electric generator that creates electricity to fire an engine's spark plugs

middle class (MID-uhl KLASS)—the group of people whose income level places them between the poor and the wealthy

riot (RYE-uht)—a group of people acting noisy, violent, and out of control

INTERNET SITES

FactHound offers a safe, fun way to find Internet sites related to this book. All of the sites on FactHound have been researched by our staff.

Here's how:
1. Visit www.facthound.com
2. Choose your grade level.
3. Type in this book ID 0736864806 for age-appropriate sites. You may also browse subjects by clicking on letters, or by clicking on pictures and words.
4. Click on the Fetch It button.

FactHound will fetch the best sites for you!

READ MORE

Bankston, John. *Henry Ford and the Assembly Line.* Unlocking the Secrets of Science. Bear, Del.: Mitchell Lane Publishers, 2004.

Ford, Carin T. *Henry Ford: The Car Man.* Famous Inventors. Berkeley Heights, N.J.: Enslow, 2003.

Parker, Lewis K. *Henry Ford and the Automobile Industry.* Reading Power. New York: PowerKids Press, 2003.

Shores, Erika L. *Henry Ford: A Photo-Illustrated Biography.* Photo-Illustrated Biographies. Mankato, Minn.: Bridgestone Books, 2004.

BIBLIOGRAPHY

Bak, Richard. *Henry and Edsel: The Creation of the Ford Empire.* Hoboken, N.J.: Wiley, 2003.

Brinkley, Douglas. *Wheels for the World: Henry Ford, His Company, and a Century of Progress, 1903–2003.* New York: Viking, 2003.

Lacey, Robert. *Ford: The Men and the Machine.* Boston: Little, Brown, 1986.

Watts, Steven. *The People's Tycoon: Henry Ford and the American Century.* New York: A. A. Knopf, 2005.

INDEX